How Can I Know What God Wants Me To Do?

Discovery Series Bible Study

Will He send me a clear signal? Will I get some kind of special feeling? How much should I rely on good old common sense? What if the Bible doesn't seem to have anything to say that applies to the matter? Why does God seem to leave me hanging in limbo when I want so desperately to hear a direct word from Him? And what about those times when there seem to be several good options, or perhaps no good option?

This study offers biblical guidelines to help us sort through the confusion and move ahead confidently through life. It is our prayer that you will discover what God wants you to do and that you will find great joy in pleasing Him.

Kurt De Haan, RBC Ministries

Publisher:	Discovery House Publishers
Editor:	David Sper
Graphic Design:	Alex Soh, Janet Chim, Ineke
Cover Photo:	Alex Soh © 2003 RBC Ministries Asia Ltd.
Series Coordinator / Study Guide:	Bill Crowder, Sim Kay Tee

This *Discovery Series Bible Study* guide is based on the *Discovery Series* booklet "How Can I Know What God Wants Me To Do?" (Q0704) from RBC Ministries. The *Discovery Series* has more than 140 titles on a variety of biblical and Christian-living issues. These 32-page booklets offer a rich resource of insight for your study of God's Word. For a catalog of *Discovery Series* booklets, write to us at: RBC Ministries, PO Box 2222, Grand Rapids, MI 49501-2222 or visit us on the Web at: www.discoveryseries.org

Discovery House Publishers

A member of the RBC Ministries family:
Our Daily Bread, Day Of Discovery, RBC Radio, Discovery Series, Campus Journal, Discovery House Music, Sports Spectrum

ISBN 1-57293-103-5

Table Of Contents

Fleeces, Fasting, And Flipping Coins

It was 5:30 a.m. and Francis Schaeffer had an agonizing decision to make. Before his father walked out the front door to go to work, he wanted to hear what his 19-year-old son was going to do.

Francis was a year out of high school and struggling to know God's will. He had put his trust in Christ as Savior the year before, and that decision had turned his life upside down. His parents wanted him to stay home and become a mechanical engineer—something Francis had wanted to do as well—but now his heart was pulling him in another direction. He sensed God leading him to go away to college to prepare for ministry.

He told his father that he needed a few more minutes to think, then he went off to the cellar to pray. He wept as he asked God for help. Finally, in desperation he took out a coin and said, "Heads, I'll go." It was heads. Then he pleaded, "God, be patient with me. If it comes up tails this time, I'll go." It was tails. "Once more, God. Please let it be heads again." It was heads.

Francis went back upstairs and told his father, "Dad, I've got to go." Although later he said he would never advise anyone else to use the same method of finding God's will, Francis felt that his decision was right (*The Tapestry* by Edith Schaeffer).

That decision was a crucial one in the life of Francis Schaeffer (1912-1984), who went on to become a pastor, the founder of L'Abri Fellowship, a philosopher, a lecturer, and an author of 24 books.

The anxiety is understandable. Even grocery shopping can be frustrating. Other decisions, like whether to rent an apartment or buy a home, seem more important. Still other actions, like selecting a college, choosing a career, picking a church to attend, and deciding who to date or who to marry, cause greater anxiety.

Then there are the heartwrenching decisions. What should you do when your spouse admits to infidelity? When a young mother is told that the infant in her womb will be severely handicapped, does she have any options? What should an employee do when he is told that if he doesn't overlook an unethical business practice he will lose his job?

Our lives can be changed forever by one decision. Add to that the tension of wanting to please God—of desiring to make the most of our lives for Him. No concerned Christian wants to choose something other than God's best. Is there a way to find out what God wants us to do in a particular situation?

The methods have been many. People have tried all kinds of tactics to determine what God wants them to do.

- fleeces (asking God for a supernatural sign)
- fasting (giving up food to seek out God)
- flipping coins (leaving it up to the toss)
- feeling (obeying feelings in spite of logic)
- floundering (fishing everywhere for answers)
- defaulting (letting events decide)
- dipping (random Bible readings)
- delegating (letting others decide for us)
- dreaming (asking for a vision or a voice)
- drawing straws (letting the length decide)
- sitting (procrastinating)
- sliding (taking the path of least resistance)
- thinking (using logic and ignoring feelings)

The confusion has been multiplying. The consequences of our decisions are often complex. Therefore, we need to gain a clear understanding of how God expects us to find our way through life. And because the Bible doesn't always give a clear answer to every question, we have to be careful how we seek solutions. But one thing is sure. We will find nothing but desperation, frustration, guilt, and uncertainty if we resort to mere human methods in our attempt to find God's will for our lives.

> **"In our quest for God's guidance, we become our own worst enemies."** —J. I. Packer

Some people have the idea that God has their lives all mapped out, but He won't show them the way. Other Christians feel guilty for past mistakes, and they resign themselves to what they think is a second-rate life. Some people tiptoe nervously through life as if they were on a tightrope. With every step they wonder if they are going to continue to receive the approval of God.

The solution is liberating. God does not intend for us to be forever frustrated and defeated, nor to have a "tightrope" mentality. There is a better way. The Bible shows us that as we do what God has clearly told us to do, He will, in His own time and way, make sure that we do not miss what He has planned for us.

How do you know that what you think you should do reflects God's wishes and not your own human desires? It can get confusing. Doing God's will isn't something that comes naturally. In Galatians 5:17 the apostle Paul wrote, "For the flesh lusts against the Spirit, and the Spirit against the flesh; and these are contrary to one another, so that you do not do the things that you wish."

Some of our confusion could be because we do not understand how God guides us. We could be giving up our own responsibility, or we could be underestimating God's involvement in our lives.

This study will show that we can know as much of God's will as we need to know, if we focus our attention on five basic principles. If we truly desire to know what God wants us to do, we cannot afford to ignore them.

Go To The Lord

Begin right. Don't wait until you are desperate or hurting before you do the most important thing. Proverbs 3:5-6 tells us, "Trust in the Lord with all your heart, and lean not on your own understanding; in all your ways acknowledge Him, and He shall direct your paths." The phrase "He shall direct your paths" can be translated more literally as "He will make your paths straight." To understand what that means, we need to look at the surrounding verses. The context (vv.1-10) describes what God will do for the person who trusts Him and follows His principles for living. Verses 5 and 6 promise that if we are living in dependence on the Lord, He will make sure that we keep on course and receive His approval.

In Psalm 5:8, David prayed, "Lead me, O Lord, in Your righteousness because of my enemies; make Your way straight before my face." David knew that God was able to show him what to do.

Why do we have to acknowledge God?

Too often we may foolishly think we are competent to make wise choices without God's help. We reason, "If God gave us brains, why is it so important to ask Him for help in making decisions?" The answer becomes obvious as we understand who God is. Because He created us, He knows us better than we know ourselves (Ps. 139:1-16). He knows everything about everything, and He understands what we will never understand (Isa. 55:8-9; Rom. 11:33-36; 1 Cor. 1:25). He is in control of everything that happens (Ps. 115:3). He is all-powerful (Jer. 32:17), and He holds us accountable to Him for our actions (vv.18-19). He wants to help us and will help us as we honor Him (Ps. 37:3-6,23-24,28). He will provide all we need now and in the life to come if we have sought Him first (Mt. 6:33). He will judge all those who thought they did not need God (Rom. 1:18-32).

How do we acknowledge the Lord?

Do we have to live at the top of a mountain, shave our heads, live in a monastery, or pray for 8 hours a day to show God that we recognize who He is? No, but there are some special ways we can acknowledge that He is in control of life's situations. We acknowledge God when we demonstrate *trust*, practice *submission*, give ourselves to *prayer*, and live in *obedience* to Him. Let's look at each of them.

What does it mean to trust Him?

Trust means that we will not depend on our own understanding (Prov. 3:5). A 2-year-old child doesn't realize how wise his parents are. He may think he knows how to operate the kitchen stove. He may wonder why Mom and Dad don't let him determine his own bedtime. But his parents "know better." As the child grows up, he would be wise to ask for their advice.

King David realized the value of trusting God when he wrote, "The Lord is my shepherd" (Ps. 23:1). Like a sheep whose life and safety depend on the shepherd, David saw that his life was in God's hands. David knew that as he followed like a sheep, the Lord would lead like a shepherd.

> **"His leading is only for those who are already committed to do as He may choose." —Lewis Sperry Chafer**

What is this about submission?

We could use the words *humble*, *reverent*, or *fearful* to describe the attitude we should possess if we want to be confident that God is leading us in our decision-making. Proverbs 1:7 reads, "The fear of the Lord is the beginning of knowledge, but fools despise wisdom and instruction." Psalm 25:9 says, "The humble He guides in justice, and the humble He teaches His way." The person who is willing to be taught will learn to please God with all decisions.

Submission is also shown through a voluntary giving up of our own desires in favor of God's desires. Romans 12:1-2 states:
I beseech you therefore, brethren, by the mercies of God, that you

present your bodies a living sacrifice, holy, acceptable to God, which is your reasonable service. And do not be conformed to this world, but be transformed by the renewing of your mind, that you may prove what is that good and acceptable and perfect will of God.

This "sacrifice" of oneself is the practical outworking of an inner attitude of submission to God. The believer who fears God will recognize His lordship over all areas of life and will relinquish any claims to self-rule. The "transformed" mind thinks in line with God's thoughts about right living. Such a transformation takes place as a believer fills his mind with the truths of God's Word. The resulting life proves that God's way is the best way to live.

How can prayer help?

The believer who trusts God and is submissive to Him recognizes his need for divine help in making decisions. The apostle James, when talking about how to handle difficulties and trials, said this:

If any of you lacks wisdom, let him ask of God, who gives to all liberally and without reproach, and it will be given to him (Jas. 1:5).

James recognized that it is not easy to know what to do when the going gets rough. So he explained that we must ask God for the needed wisdom. Decisions are often necessary as our faith is tested or as we endure a trial. In a wider application, James 1:5 promises that God will give help to all who ask Him.

> **"Don't expect God to reveal His will for you next week until you practice it for today."** —**Alan Redpath**

Failure to ask for God's direction can be a sign of arrogance. Although we may feel confident in ourselves, God knows the bigger picture. The danger of not consulting God is illustrated in Joshua 9. When Israel was in the process of conquering the land of Palestine, the Gibeonites tried to trick Israel into making a peace treaty with them. Israel rushed into a decision without asking God. Verse 14 states that the men of Israel "did not ask counsel of the Lord." They didn't think they needed to ask God about something that seemed to make so much sense—

yet they were wrong. They ended up making a treaty with people the Lord had ordered Israel to kill.

An example of the value of prayer in seeking God's will is found in Colossians. The apostle Paul prayed for the Colossian believers, asking that they "may be filled with the knowledge of His will in all wisdom and spiritual understanding; that [they] may walk worthy of the Lord, fully pleasing Him, being fruitful in every good work and increasing in the knowledge of God" (1:9-10).

God *does* reveal His will to us. Through His Word and through the indwelling Spirit we have all the resources we need. But first we must pray.

What if we don't do what we know we should?

Why should God give a person guidance on some specific situation in life if that person shows contempt or disregard for God in another area of life? The central issue is whether or not we are walking in obedience to what we already know God wants us to do. Why should we expect God to show—through circumstances, people, or the inner work of the Holy Spirit—what He wants us to do, if we do not fully intend to obey Him?

> **Why should we expect God to show—
> through circumstances, people, or the inner work
> of the Holy Spirit—what He wants us to do,
> if we do not fully intend to obey Him?**

Consider the example of Jonah. He was clearly told by God to go to Nineveh, but he ran the other way. Would you expect God to give Jonah direction on a new career choice? I doubt it.

What can we expect if we acknowledge Him?

We can certainly expect God to honor His promise to help us. He will give us everything we need in order to know what to do. That doesn't mean God will spell out everything for us when in fact He has already given us the scriptural principles to use in making our decisions. Or He may expect us to use our ability to reason as a guide in choosing a path that would be in keeping with His general guidelines. In any case, we can expect God to give us the direction we need. He is in control of all of life (Eph. 1:11). As we seek His will, He will work out His plan through us (Phil. 2:13).

Even if we have failed to acknowledge Him in the past, we can fulfill His will for us today and tomorrow as we learn to acknowledge Him in our lives.

What does the Holy Spirit do for us?

Jesus promised that the Spirit would live within believers (Jn. 14:15-18; 16:7-15). But what is the Spirit doing to lead us in our decision-making? His main role is to help us understand what God has already revealed in the Bible (see 1 Cor. 2:6-16).

There are also several New Testament examples of how the Holy Spirit can work through inner impressions (Acts 8:29; 11:28; 13:2; 21:11; 1 Cor. 14:30). A word of warning, though, is needed. Impressions can be deceiving. And impressions can come from questionable sources: our selfish desires, mental baggage from the past, or even satanic delusion. So we can't put all our hope for guidance on subjective feelings. That's why it is so important to look for biblical principles that the Spirit can use to give us unmistakable direction.

How Can I Know
What To Do?

Go To
The Lord

Matthew 6:33—"Seek first
the kingdom of God and
His righteousness, and all
these things shall be
added to you."

Objective:
**To establish
the wisdom of
trusting God for
His guidance in
our lives.**

Bible Memorization:
Matthew 6:33

Read:
**"Go To The Lord"
pp.7-11**

Warming Up
List some of the methods you have used to determine
God's will. Which was your favorite? Which was the
most bizarre? Which was the most effective? Why?

Thinking Through
According to page 5, "Our lives can be changed forever
by one decision." What are some of the decisions you
have made that have changed your life significantly?

Consider the quote on page 6: "In our quest for God's
guidance, we become our own worst enemies." What
did J. I. Packer mean by that? Has this been true in
your own experience?

"God does reveal His will to us. Through His Word and
through the indwelling Spirit we have all the resources
we need. But first we must pray" (p.10). Why, then, are
so many Christians confused about God's will for their
lives? Do you think it's more a matter of "not praying,"
"not knowing," or "not obeying"?

Digging In
Key Text: Proverbs 3:5-6
What does it mean for us to "trust in the Lord" and to
"acknowledge Him"? Why does it make good sense for
us to trust God for His guidance?

What does verse 5 mean when it says "lean not on your own understanding." Does this mean that we're to ignore common sense? What is the role of common sense in determining God's will?

The phrase "all your ways" is so comprehensive that it can be unsettling. Why are we often reluctant to submit "all" to God's purposes? How would you compare the "all" in this passage to the one in Romans 8:28? What connection do you see between them?

Going Further
Refer
What Bible characters can you think of who practiced the wisdom of Proverbs 3:5-6? In what ways did they "trust in" and "acknowledge" the Lord? How was it evident that they weren't relying on their "own understanding"? How did God direct their lives?

Reflect
Have you acknowledged the Lord in all areas of your life? Why would it be foolish to ask God to guide you in making an important decision in one area of life if you are ignoring what He has said about other areas of life? If you have not consistently prayed for God's direction, begin now to seek His wisdom for life.

"⁵Trust in the Lord with all your heart, and lean not on your own understanding; ⁶in all your ways acknowledge Him, and He shall direct your paths."
Proverbs 3:5-6

"We know that all things work together for good to those who love God, to those who are the called according to His purpose."
Romans 8:28

Understand His Principles

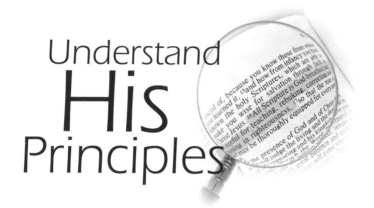

If you didn't know how to play a board game like *Monopoly*, how would you learn? You could ask someone to explain it to you, or you could go directly to the rulebook yourself, because rules can be misinterpreted or forgotten by other players. The final word is always the rulebook, written by the inventor of the game.

But what about something much more complex—like life itself? As the Inventor of life, God has spelled out how we are to "play the game." And we aren't allowed to make up our own rules to fit our own preferences. In life, the rulebook is the Bible, and it covers all the big issues. It contains everything we need to know about right thinking and right living (2 Tim. 3:16-17). But it does not speak directly to many issues that come up as we encounter complex situations. So what do we do? We need to understand (a) what the Bible clearly says, and (b) how its principles can apply to all situations of life to give us guidance. But we have to be careful that we do not misuse God's Word.

> **"My grace is sufficient for you,
> for My strength is made perfect in weakness."**
> **—2 Corinthians 12:9**

How is the Bible misused?

A classic story is told of one way the Bible has been misused to find guidance. It's about the young man who used the "flip and point" method of reading the Bible. One day while wondering what to do with his life, he flipped his Bible open and pointed to Matthew 27:5. He read, "[Judas] went and hanged himself." He thought maybe he should try again. So he flipped and pointed, this time landing on Luke 10:37, "Go and do likewise." He tried flipping one more time and arrived at John 13:27, "What you do, do quickly." We may laugh at the absurdity of such a method of trying to determine God's will, yet we are often guilty of treating the Bible in a similar way. The Bible, however, is not a Christian Ouija board.

Most of the favorite methods of Bible misuse fall into the general category of taking verses out of context. Whether the method is flipping and pointing, taking for yourself messages directed toward someone else, or the more simple "reading into the text" a message that is not really there, the problem is the same—mishandling the Scriptures.

What does the Bible clearly say?

Too many times we are guilty of not considering what the Bible says on an issue. For example, you don't have to wonder if God wants you to leave your spouse to marry another person you find attractive. Jesus said that marriage is a lifetime commitment (Mt. 19:6).

God has spelled out all we need to know. The Old Testament people of God were told, "The secret things belong to the Lord our God, but those things which are revealed belong to us and to our children forever, that we may do all the words of this law" (Dt. 29:29). The Israelites were not to occupy their time trying to find out God's secrets about His future plan and purposes in the world, but they were responsible to obey what God had clearly revealed. The same truth can be applied to us. We cannot know or understand all that God is doing in our world. But we can understand our responsibilities before Him. Those duties are spelled out in God's Word. The Bible clearly tells us:

- Worship God, not idols (Ex. 20:3-4).
- Honor your parents (Eph. 6:1-3).
- Do not murder (Ex. 20:13).
- Do not commit adultery (Heb. 13:4).

- Do not lie (Ex. 20:16; Eph. 4:15,25).
- Do not covet (Ex. 20:17; Rom. 7:7-8).
- Do not lust (Mt. 5:27-28).
- Forgive others (Mk. 11:25; Eph. 4:32).
- Love God and your neighbor (Mk. 12:28-31).
- Be holy (1 Pet. 1:16).
- Do not marry an unbeliever (1 Cor. 7:39; 2 Cor. 6:14-15).
- Help a brother in need (1 Jn. 3:16-19).
- Don't take a Christian to court (1 Cor. 6:1-8).
- Do not steal (Eph. 4:28).
- Be reconciled quickly to the person with whom you have a dispute (Mt. 5:23-24).
- Tell the truth (Prov. 12:22).

The list could go on and on, but the point is this: The Bible is full of God's clear commands that offer us direction for most of life's decisions. The more we know of God's written Word, the more quickly we will know what God wants us to do.

"The will of God is found in the Word of God. The more a person grows, the more he begins to think instinctively and habitually from a divine perspective." —Howard Hendricks

Ephesians 5:17 states, "Do not be unwise, but understand what the will of the Lord is." The Lord's will is clear, as Paul stated in the preceding verses: "See then that you walk circumspectly, not as fools but as wise, redeeming the time, because the days are evil" (vv.15-16). God's clear will for our lives is that we live for Him and obey Him in all we do. We are not to live as unbelievers but as children of God who obey His commands for holy living (Eph. 4:17–5:17).

What if the matter isn't so clear?

Many areas of life are not addressed by the clear commands of God's Word. The Bible doesn't tell us which television programs are acceptable viewing. It doesn't tell us what kind of music to listen to. It doesn't have a command that tells us what to do on Saturday nights. There isn't a specific command that says, "Don't buy lottery tickets." If you are looking for guidance on whether to buy granola or jelly-filled donuts, the Bible doesn't say which to buy. And it doesn't tell us specifically how to spend our paychecks. But that doesn't mean that we are left entirely on our own. It is in those areas that God offers general guidelines in His Word. For example, the Bible offers these principles:

- Don't try to get rich quick (Prov. 28:22).
- Put your treasures in heaven (Mt. 6:20).
- Don't follow the crowd (Rom. 12:1-2).
- Be subject to authorities (Rom. 13:1-4).
- Choose the best (Phil. 4:8).
- Work for God, not your boss (Col. 3:23).
- Be faithful (1 Cor. 4:2).
- Don't be enslaved (1 Cor. 6:12).
- Treat your body as God's temple (1 Cor. 6:19-20).
- Glorify God in everything (1 Cor. 10:31).
- Live by grace, not legalism (Gal. 5:1-6).
- Don't give Satan opportunity (Eph. 4:27).
- Use your tongue to edify (Eph. 4:29).
- Seek the good of others (Phil. 2:3-4).
- Work hard (1 Th. 4:11-12).

These are only a few of the many principles that come from God's Word. Personal study and learning from gifted teachers will help us discover the biblical guidelines we should implement in our lives.

STUDY NO. 2

How Can I Know
What To Do?

Understand
His Principles

Ephesians 5:17—"Do
not be unwise, but
understand what the
will of the Lord is."

Objective:
**To understand
the biblical
guidelines for
making decisions.**

Bible Memorization:
Ephesians 5:17

Read:
**"Understand His
Principles"
pp.14-17**

Warming Up
It's important to use the Bible in decision-making, but it
has often been misused. Give an example of someone
who claimed that the Bible was the basis for wrong
actions or attitudes?

Thinking Through
"Too many times we are guilty of not considering what
the Bible says on an issue" (p.15). Recount a decision
you made knowing it was contrary to what the Bible
teaches. What were the results of that decision?

On page 16 we read that "the Bible is full of God's clear
commands and principles that offer us direction for
most of life's decisions." Why, then, don't we read and
study the Bible more than we do?

What's the difference between a biblical command and
a biblical principle? Why is this difference important?
What examples of biblical commands and principles
(other than those listed on pp.15-17) can you find?

Digging In
Key Text: 2 Timothy 3:16-17
What is meant by the word *inspiration* in verse 16?
How does God's inspiration of the Bible affect our
attitude and obedience toward its teaching?

In this passage, Paul said that Scripture is profitable for four things. What are they? What does each one mean? How are they different? What are the implications of each one?

What is the ultimate purpose of the Scriptures in a believer's life? How is the word *complete* defined in part by the phrase "thoroughly equipped for every good work"?

"[16]All Scripture is given by inspiration of God, and is profitable for doctrine, for reproof, for correction, for instruction in righteousness, [17]that the man of God may be complete, thoroughly equipped for every good work."
2 Timothy 3:16-17

Going Further
Refer
In light of Deuteronomy 29:29, will God always reveal His plans to us? Why would He choose to reveal certain things to us yet not reveal other things? What should be our response to those "secret things" He has not revealed?

"The secret things belong to the Lord our God, but those things which are revealed belong to us and to our children forever, that we may do all the words of this law."
Deuteronomy 29:29

Reflect
What are some specific biblical guidelines you have applied to your life during this past week? Are you feeding your thoughts with God's Word? If you are not already doing so, set aside a daily time to search out instruction from the Bible.

Investigate Your Options

Imagine that you are enjoying a peaceful swim in the ocean when you suddenly see a shark's fin moving in your direction. You have several options. You could ignore it. You could swim toward it and try to kill it with your bare hands. You could head for shore, trying not to draw its attention. Or you could try to pet the shark and become its friend.

Obviously, some options are not too wise. Trying to kill the shark, attempting to be its pal, or ignoring the approaching jaws probably wouldn't work. The best option would be to head quickly for shore without attracting its interest.

Granted, in such a situation you wouldn't take time to list all available options, even the absurd ones. But you would quickly assess the situation and determine an escape plan based on your existing knowledge of sharks.

Knowing your options is important for making all kinds of decisions. Although the first option you come across may seem right, other choices must be considered. First impressions do not necessarily give you an accurate picture (Prov. 18:17).

What are the consequences of each alternative?

It is not enough to lay out the options. We must also consider the probable results of each action. If the problem is an approaching shark, the consequences of each alternative would help determine your decision. In other matters, like trying to decide what college to attend or what job to take, listing the implications of each choice can be very helpful. For example, if choosing one job means having to move away from family and friends or means a dramatic pay cut, that may be a significant reason to pursue another job opportunity. And don't forget to consider the spiritual impact your decision will have on you and those around you.

How can God use our minds?

It may not seem as spiritual to say that you chose job opportunity "A" over job "B" because of social and financial reasons as it is to say "the Lord led me" to job "A." But it is probably just as true—and a little less presumptuous. God often does lead us through the use of good judgment. After all, He did give us a brain to use and a lot of available information. If you already have the information close at hand, why should God drop a road sign from the sky?

For example, if you are trying to decide what kind of shoes to buy, God expects you to use your head. It wouldn't be wise to waste money on shoes with an inflated price, nor would it be wise to buy shoes in some wild color that you would never wear. You would be wise to choose shoes that are comfortable, durable, and affordable.

A biblical example of this principle can be found in the life of the early church. In Acts 6:2-4, Luke told of the apostles' wise decision to look for help in taking care of food distribution when the task was distracting them from accomplishing their Christ-appointed ministries. It made sense to choose godly men who would be able to share the workload.

> **"God gave you an awful lot of leading when He gave you your mind."** —Dawson Trotman

In 1 Corinthians 2, the apostle Paul spoke of how the Spirit of God works in the minds of believers to give them the ability to grasp God's truths. In verse 16, Paul said of believers, "We have the mind of Christ." The Spirit guides us in understanding the Bible, but He also transforms us in action and thought to be more like Christ. We can be sure that as we obey the Lord and depend on Him, the Spirit of God will assist us, even in developing a godly common sense about life's decisions.

Good judgment, then, is a tool God expects us to use in making decisions, whether simple or complex. When joined with a daily dependence on the Lord, our God-given reasoning ability can be a helpful guide as we choose between alternatives.

What are the unique aspects of your situation?

No two people are the same, nor are the situations in which they must make decisions. Granted, in those areas of life spoken to directly by the Bible's commands, it doesn't matter who you are. The right choice is always to obey what the Bible says to do. But in those decisions of life about which the Bible does not clearly address the issues, and when the principles don't seem to apply, a different approach is necessary. In those situations it is important to list the options and alternatives and to take note of the unique aspects of your situation. For example, Joe may have decided to ask Marianne to be his wife, but that certainly doesn't mean Bob should too! Simply because Fred thought State U. was the best place for him to go to school does not mean it would necessarily be best for Sam or Sandra. Just because a mature Christian you highly respect has chosen to attend a particular church does not mean you should go to that church as well.

Every person is different. If we fail to recognize those differences, we will make decisions on the basis of what others have done instead of what would be wise for us to do.

**If we fail to recognize our differences,
we will make decisions on the basis of what others
have done instead of what would be wise for us to do.**

What are your abilities, gifts, talents, and weaknesses?

If you have never learned how to use a typewriter, would it be wise for you to apply for a job as a typist? If you have never driven a car over 55 miles per hour, would it be advisable to apply as a driver for the Indianapolis 500? If you break out in hives when you have to speak in front of people, would it be smart for you to run for political office? If you don't know the difference between a socket wrench and a spatula, would it be smart for you to interview for a job as an auto mechanic or a chef? If you have a weight problem and have difficulty refusing the temptation of chocolates, should you take a job in a candy-bar factory where employees can eat all they want? Or if you don't enjoy teaching the Bible or counseling, should you pursue a church pastorate?

The answer to all these questions is *no*. It only makes good sense that what God wants you to do He has equipped and prepared you to do. For example, a person who does not fit the requirements of 1 Timothy 3:1-7 and Titus 1:5-9 and shows no evidence that he has been divinely equipped by God to be a pastor-teacher (Eph. 4:11) should not think that God wants him to be a church pastor. Likewise, in any opportunity that comes your way, evaluate your abilities, interests, and even your weaknesses to find good information for deciding what God wants you to do.

STUDY NO. 3

How Can I Know
What To Do?

Investigate Your Options

1 Corinthians 2:16—"For 'who has known the mind of the Lord that he may instruct Him?' But we have the mind of Christ."

Objective:
To learn how to personally work through the decision-making process.

Bible Memorization:
1 Corinthians 2:16

Read:
**"Investigate Your Options"
pp.20-23**

Warming Up
In making a decision, are you more likely to be influenced by how you feel (your heart) or by what you think (your mind)? Why?

Thinking Through
Why is it unwise to make decisions that are based on first impressions? (see p.20). How can careful investigation protect us from our own inclinations?

Consider the quote by Dawson Trotman on page 21: "God gave you an awful lot of leading when He gave you your mind." What does this mean? How does this relate to our earlier consideration of Proverbs 3:5-6?

When using your mind to determine God's will, what are some of the factors that must be considered? In what ways are your particular circumstances, training, abilities, strengths and weaknesses, gifts, talents, personality, and disposition important considerations?

Digging In
Key Text: Acts 6:2-4
In your own words, describe the situation that was bringing conflict to the Jerusalem church. Describe the steps used in this passage for reaching a solution and the priorities that helped shape that solution.

According to verse 3, the apostles were to look for men who were "full of the Holy Spirit and wisdom." In what ways do these qualities work together to make someone a good leader?

What does this passage tell us about the priority the apostles placed on the study of the Word of God and prayer?

Going Further
Refer
Read 1 Corinthians 2:12-16. In light of this passage, what is the role of the Holy Spirit in guiding believers to godly wisdom?

Reflect
Evaluate a major decision you have made recently. List each of the alternatives and their consequences. Did your decision violate any biblical principles? Did it violate good judgment? Which alternatives would have made a positive impact on your spiritual well-being? Which of the remaining ones would you be inclined to select? Why?

"²Then the twelve summoned the multitude of the disciples and said, 'It is not desirable that we should leave the Word of God and serve tables. ³Therefore, brethren, seek out from among you seven men of good reputation, full of the Holy Spirit and wisdom, whom we may appoint over this business; ⁴but we will give ourselves continually to prayer and to the ministry of the Word.'"
Acts 6:2-4

"¹²Now we have received, not the spirit of the world, but the Spirit who is from God, that we might know the things that have been freely given to us by God. ¹³These things we also speak, not in words which man's wisdom teaches but which the Holy Spirit teaches, comparing spiritual things with spiritual. ¹⁴But the natural man does not receive the things of the Spirit of God, for they are foolishness to him; nor can he know them, because they are spiritually discerned. ¹⁵But he who is spiritual judges all things, yet he himself is rightly judged by no one. ¹⁶For 'who has known the mind of the Lord that he may instruct Him?' But we have the mind of Christ."
1 Corinthians 2:12-16

Discuss It With Others

Driving a car through a maze of unfamiliar streets can be unsettling. But it can also be a challenge to one's ego and a test of the strength of a marriage or friendship. Many drivers (including me) dislike stopping and asking for help—even when it is obviously needed. Often, though, a passenger (wife, husband, or friend) pleads that the driver stop and ask someone for directions. Many headaches, many extra miles, and many strained relationships could be avoided if the driver simply followed good advice and asked for help. The same is true spiritually.

Why do I need to listen to others?

The answer seems obvious, but we often fail at this very point. Whether it is an overinflated ego, overconfidence, "adviceophobia," or simply failure to understand the wisdom others have to offer, we foolishly refuse to ask for directions. And we suffer the consequences. We can learn so much if we are just willing to listen to others.

What can I learn from other people?

First-time home buyers can experience much anxiety trying to decide what home to purchase. What is a good deal and how should it all be financed? A person would be foolish to buy the first home he saw listed in the newspaper without seeing it, or without getting sound advice from experts in home sales. In such a decision, the advice of others is invaluable. It can mean the difference between getting stuck with high mortgage payments for a piece of decaying junk and buying a well-constructed affordable home that will increase in value.

Solomon wrote, "The way of a fool is right in his own eyes, but he who heeds counsel is wise" (Prov. 12:15). Others can see what we cannot, and they can be more objective in their evaluation of issues that to us are highly charged. They can point out errors in our judgment and add valuable insights.

Do I have to take advice when it is given?

Of course not. Human advice is not a command from God. Some advice is better than others. Some people who give advice are more knowledgeable. And simply because more people advise one course of action over another is not enough reason to move in that direction. Many other factors may be involved. In fact, we may receive contradictory advice. Then we have to decide who is worth listening to.

> **"Don't be a spiritual lone-ranger; when you think you see God's will, have your perception checked. Draw on the wisdom of those who are wiser than you are. Take advice."** —J. I. Packer

Whose advice should I seek?

If you want some tips on how to navigate a submarine, it wouldn't make much sense to ask a person who has never even seen one. And if you are trying to decide how to choose a marriage partner, you don't ask someone who has been divorced 10 times. We need to seek out those people who have reliable information. Not only do we need information, but we also need godly counsel from people who are in tune with God, who are sensitive to the spiritual issues, and who know how to apply the Lord's wisdom to the many aspects of life.

The first two verses of Psalm 1 remind us of the need for the right kind of advice.

Blessed is the man who walks not in the counsel of the ungodly, nor stands in the path of sinners, nor sits in the seat of the scornful; but his delight is in the law of the Lord, and in His law he meditates day and night.

Rehoboam was the grandson of David, Israel's greatest king. He should have learned from his grandfather where to go for advice. When his father Solomon died, Rehoboam became Israel's king. But instead of following the wise and mature counsel of his father's friends, he went along with the advice of his young contemporaries who lacked the godly wisdom of the elders (2 Chr. 10). As a result, Rehoboam lost a large part of his kingdom. He made the mistake of looking for someone who agreed with his opinion instead of listening to wisdom. People today continue to make the same kind of mistake.

When we seek out advice, we must do so with an openness to being corrected or to having our initial choice rethought. It does little good to ask for advice when our mind is already made up.

STUDY
NO. 4

How Can I Know
What To Do?

Discuss It
With Others

Proverbs 12:15—"The
way of a fool is right in
his own eyes, but he
who heeds counsel is
wise."

Objective:
**To understand the
value of wise
counsel from other
believers.**

Bible Memorization:
Proverbs 12:15

Read:
**"Discuss It With
Others"
pp.27-29**

Warming Up
When you have to talk to someone about an important decision, whom do you go to? Why do you value that person's input?

Thinking Through
What are the advantages of asking other people for advice when you have to make a decision? What are the disadvantages? The limitations? The dangers?

What kind of qualities do you look for in an advisor? How many advisors would you consult before you felt ready to make a decision? Why? Do you place more value on the quality or the quantity of your advisors?

What would you do if you received contrary advice from two different advisors, both of whom you value and trust? What would you do if the advice from a majority vote of your advisors was contrary to God's Word and/or contrary to how you would have decided?

Digging In
Key Text: Psalm 1
Who are the "ungodly," the "sinners," and the "scornful" in Psalm 1? Are they non-Christians or wicked people? Why does the psalmist say it is a blessing not to take the advice of such people?

As a Christian, should you go to a non-Christian for advice? In what types of decisions would this be appropriate? Inappropriate? How does this relate to Psalm 1:1?

What is the "law of the Lord," and how do you "delight" in it? What does it mean to "meditate" in His law "day and night"? How would a delight in and meditation on the Scriptures protect you from wrong counsel?

Going Further
Refer
Write your own paraphrase of Proverbs 19:20-21. In this proverb, the plans of man are contrasted with the Lord's counsel. How can you tell the difference?

Reflect
Why can it be dangerous to base your decision on a majority vote of your advisors? Have you made wise use of counsel in the past? Do you take advice well? Why would it be profitable to do your own research first before seeking the suggestions of others?

"[1]Blessed is the man who walks not in the counsel of the ungodly, nor stands in the path of sinners, nor sits in the seat of the scornful; [2]but his delight is in the law of the Lord, and in His law he meditates day and night. [3]He shall be like a tree planted by the rivers of water, that brings forth its fruit in its season, whose leaf also shall not wither; and whatever he does shall prosper. [4]The ungodly are not so, but are like the chaff which the wind drives away. [5]Therefore the ungodly shall not stand in the judgment, nor sinners in the congregation of the righteous. [6]For the Lord knows the way of the righteous, but the way of the ungodly shall perish."
Psalm 1

"[20]Listen to counsel and receive instruction, that you may be wise in your latter days. [21]There are many plans in a man's heart, nevertheless the Lord's counsel— that will stand."
Proverbs 19:20-21

Express Your Freedom

Should you be deeply concerned about whether you wear red socks or blue? Is it necessary to pray about it, search for a biblical theology of colors, and seek the advice of your pastor? If you say *yes*, your life must be miserable! God did not intend for us to be frozen in anxiety each time we have to make a choice.

How free are we?

God gave freedom to use our own heads to decide what to do. Consider Adam, for example. God put him in the Garden of Eden and told him to name the animals (Gen. 2:19-20). Did Adam get all flustered and say, "But Lord, I want to make sure I name them exactly what You think they should be named"? No, God gave Adam freedom to choose the names that pleased Adam, and it was fine with God.

Another example from Genesis 2 was Adam's choice of food. God had said that Adam could eat from any tree he wanted, except for one. That gave Adam great freedom—even though later he and Eve overextended their freedom and disobeyed God. And therein lies the key. Our God-given freedom extends to those decisions that God's commands and principles have not addressed.

For example, a fish in the ocean is free to swim anywhere it wants to flap its fins. But if it chose to flip up onto land, the decision would be fatal. As human beings, we have freedom to choose among good options that conform to God's standards and His ideas of wisdom. Once we "jump out" of God's standards, however, we make a major mistake.

How does this work in real life?

Will it violate a biblical principle if I buy a Cadillac instead of a Ford? It would if I trampled all over my wife's feelings on the matter (violation of the principle of Ephesians 5:25-33), or if my decision meant that my children wouldn't have food on the table because my loan payments were too high (violation of the principle of 1 Timothy 5:8). On the other hand, my choice of cars could be an area where I have a great deal of freedom without violating a biblical principle. There could be several good choices that meet God's standards and reflect a wise use of my God-given mental ability.

If in doubt, is it wise to wait?

If you are standing in line at a fast-food restaurant wondering whether to have a hamburger or a cheeseburger, the outcome of your decision isn't likely to be life-changing. But when the person behind the counter says, "May I help you," you have to come up with a decision or else get out of line. It would be ridiculous to agonize over such a choice. But what about bigger decisions like proposing marriage, choosing a vocation, deciding whether or not to have risky surgery, or determining how to care for a relative who is terminally ill? At times it may be wise to wait—if you have the luxury of extra time and if waiting will allow you to find valuable new information or allow for a better analysis of facts already available. Haste is not a virtue (Prov. 21:5).

> **"The Bible does not provide a map for life—only a compass."** —Haddon Robinson

If we are extremely uneasy about a decision, we should take time to evaluate why we feel that way. In some cases, such lack of peace may indicate that our choice is "not from faith" and is a sinful violation of our conscience (Rom. 14:23). Or a lack of peace may indicate that we have not expressed our trust in God to meet our needs (Phil. 4:6-7).

We should remember that although God can use our feelings to direct us, what we "feel" may be a result of our emotional makeup rather than a message from God's Spirit. And watch out for the paralysis of analysis, a decision-crippling disease affecting those who procrastinate or who continually fear that some bit of information is yet to be found that will help them know what God wants them to do.

Could I flip a coin?

In some cases, yes. Does that sound a bit unspiritual? It isn't if you have acknowledged the Lord, looked for principles in His Word, used common sense, and listened to good advice. Flipping a coin, though, or making an arbitrary choice should be a last resort, and only when you are choosing between good options.

In Proverbs 16:33, Solomon said, "The lot is cast into the lap, but its every decision is from the Lord." Casting lots, drawing straws, or flipping a coin fall into the same category. In the Bible, God worked through such techniques to reveal what He wanted done. For example:

- Aaron cast lots on the Day of Atonement to select a goat to sacrifice (Lev. 16:8-10).
- Nehemiah used lot-casting to distribute work responsibilities (Neh. 10:34).
- Solomon said that casting lots could stop people from fighting (Prov. 18:18).
- Jonah was discovered as the villain when a ship captain cast the lot (Jon. 1:7).
- Matthias was chosen by lot as an apostle when a replacement was needed (Acts 1:23-26).

> **"It is God who works in you both to will and to do for His good pleasure."** —Philippians 2:13

When all available information yields no clear direction and a decision is needed, use your God-given freedom of choice or, if paralyzed by indecision, simply flip a coin. God can use either choice for His glory. He is in control and He is at work in the lives of those who earnestly desire to please Him.

How does our freedom fit into the bigger picture?

It's important that we see our freedom of choice in the context of all that God has offered to help us know what He wants us to do. He hasn't left us out in the middle of a wilderness without a compass. He offers help to all who will acknowledge Him as Lord. He has given us reliable guidance in His Word. He has given us rational thinking power to evaluate our options. We have information in the form of advice from people we can trust. And He gives us freedom to choose when the decision lacks any clear admonition or prohibition from Him.

> **If we desire to honor God, we can be sure
> that He will not leave us in the dark when we want
> to know what He wants us to do.**

God loves us. He wants us to live for Him. If we desire to honor God, we can be sure that He will not leave us in the dark when we want to know what He wants us to do. Even if we have been foolish or disobedient in the past, we can know and do what God wants us to do—today and tomorrow.

Summarizing the principles

We have seen that we can know as much of God's will as we need to know—if we focus our attention on five basic principles. To remember these principles more easily, we have formed an acrostic using the first letter of each one to spell the word *GUIDE*. It looks like this:

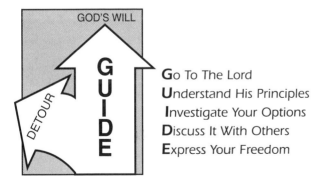

Go To The Lord
Understand His Principles
Investigate Your Options
Discuss It With Others
Express Your Freedom

STUDY
NO. **5**

How Can I Know
What To Do?

Express Your Freedom

Philippians 2:13—"It is God who works in you both to will and to do for His good pleasure."

Objective.
To develop the ability to exercise our Christian liberty as part of the decision-making process.

Bible Memorization:
Philippians 2:13

Read:
"Express Your Freedom" pp.32-35

Warming Up
Would it be right or wrong for a Christian to spend $250,000 on a luxury car? Why? How would you decide if it were God's will for you to buy such an expensive car?

Thinking Through
Why is it wise to wait to make a decision if you're in doubt? (see p.33). What are the dangers of impulsive decisions? What's wrong with the "paralysis of analysis"? What should you do during a time of waiting? What should you do if you don't have the luxury of extra time?

Is having a sense of peace a reliable indicator of being in God's will, or is it dangerous to rely on this? (see p.33). Why?

Is it wrong or sinful to flip a coin to determine God's will? (see p.34). Why or why not? Can God lead us into His will with the flip of a coin, or is this toying with chance? How would you defend your answer?

Digging In
Key Text: Genesis 2:16-20
What decisions and freedom of choices were given to Adam? How did he exercise his freedom?

Why would God provide the "tree of the knowledge of good and evil," and then prohibit Adam from eating of it?

What does this passage teach us about the freedom and the limits of choices that God gives to us? Why do you think God gives us the freedom to make choices? Why does He set limits on that freedom?

Going Further
Refer
Consider 1 Corinthians 6:12. What did Paul mean when he said that "all things are lawful"? What is the extent of freedom that God has given to us? Give some examples of things that are permissible but not necessarily beneficial.

Reflect
What kinds of decisions do you make every day without prayer and study to find out what to do? What kinds of decisions give you the most anxiety and tend to paralyze you? Are you exercising your freedom responsibly and in dependence on the Lord?

"[16]And the Lord God commanded the man, saying, 'Of every tree of the garden you may freely eat; [17]but of the tree of the knowledge of good and evil you shall not eat, for in the day that you eat of it you shall surely die.' [18]And the Lord God said, 'It is not good that man should be alone; I will make him a helper comparable to him.' [19]Out of the ground the Lord God formed every beast of the field and every bird of the air, and brought them to Adam to see what he would call them. And whatever Adam called each living creature, that was its name. [20]So Adam gave names to all cattle, to the birds of the air, and to every beast of the field. But for Adam there was not found a helper comparable to him."
Genesis 2:16-20

"All things are lawful for me, but all things are not helpful. All things are lawful for me, but I will not be brought under the power of any."
1 Corinthians 6:12

Quiet Nudges

By Philip Yancey

I have thought through some of the key events of my recent life, searching for threads of guidance. I refer to them not as examples of yet another technique, but as illustrations of the quiet nudges God can use to guide us without overwhelming us.

I have a confession to make. For me, at least, guidance only becomes evident when I look backward, months and years later. Then, the circuitous process falls into place and the hand of God seems clear. But at the moment of decision, I feel mainly confusion and uncertainty. Indeed, almost all the guidance in my life has been subtle and indirect.

I think, for example, of a major crossroad in my career. While working for *Campus Life* magazine, I felt the constant tug between two irreconcilable directions. One pulled me toward management, business, marketing, budgeting; the other toward editorial directing and writing. For many months, I tried both, unable to decide. Each field offered ministry opportunities, similar rewards, and equal appeal. I enjoyed both roles. Most advisors counseled me toward the management role because of the organization's needs. I often prayed about the decision but never received any concrete guidance.

Over time, I began to notice a trend, however: a battle with insomnia. Externally, I handled the pressures of management well and stayed healthy to all appearances. But often I would have bouts of insomnia, so severe that I would get only 1 or 2 hours of sleep at night. It took me almost a year to notice a further detail: I slept well when I worked on writing projects; I could not sleep when I worked in management. I tried to ignore the signs for another few months, but they became almost comically evident (if insomnia can ever be considered comical).

For a time I would work one full week on writing projects, then one full week on management. It was true. I slept like a baby (truthfully, more like a colicky baby) during writing weeks and slept hardly at all during management weeks. Could this be divine guidance? I wondered. I had heard of God speaking through dreams, but through insomnia?

The situation never changed, and finally I concluded the message of insomnia was as direct a form of guidance as I would get. Now that I look back on it, it seems startlingly direct.

> **For me, guidance only becomes evident when I look back months and years later.**

I also think of the circumstances that led to some of the books I have written. *Where Is God When It Hurts?* came out of a rejection. Back in 1975, I had what I thought to be a wonderful idea for a book. I had just discovered *Devotions*, by John Donne, a meditation in 23 parts, written while Donne lay with a terminal illness. The concepts were superb, but the King James-era English made the content impenetrable to many modern readers. I wrote several publishers, proposing to do for *Devotions* what Ken Taylor had done for the King James Version—a *Living Donne*, perhaps, or *John Donne Redone*. I spent long hours working up samples. Everyone judged the idea fine as a literary exercise but totally unmarketable as a contemporary book.

My boss at that time had a suggestion. "The problem," he said, "is not just the dated language, but the dated context and even dated way of thinking. Why don't you do your own book on the problem of pain and suffering, using modern examples?" *Where Is God When It Hurts?* was born.

While researching for that book, I met Paul Brand, a world authority on the subject of pain. I came to know him "by chance," when my wife cleaned out a supply closet at the warehouse of a Christian relief organization.

"There's an article on pain in this international conference report that I think you'll like," she told me. Dr. Brand's unique perspective in this report so fascinated me that I arranged for a meeting as soon as possible. During our conversations, I ultimately learned of a scruffed-up transcript of some devotional talks he had kept in a file drawer for 20 years. That transcript became the genesis of *Fearfully And Wonderfully Made*.

As I look back, the hand of God seems evident in those and many other choices. They fit together into a pattern. But at the time, they seemed no more extraordinary than any other event in my life: a rejection slip on a book idea, a musty book from a supply closet, a set of devotional talks given in India by a stranger 20 years before.

This pattern has recurred so often (and clear guidance for the future has occurred so seldom) that I am about to conclude that we have a basic direction wrong. I had always thought of guidance as forward-looking. We keep praying, hoping, counting on God to reveal what we should do next. In my own experience, at least, I have found the direction to be reversed. The focus must be on the moment before me, the present. How is my relationship to God? As circumstances change, for better or worse, will I respond with obedience and trust?

For me, guidance becomes clear only as I look backward. At the moment, my future is a big blur. My present is a daily struggle to crank out more words and a desire to grow in relationship with God.

A picture is being painted, for me, for all who are called the sons and daughters of God. Yet it does not take shape until enough time passes for me to stand up and look back on what colors and designs have been laid down. If I saw the pattern in advance, a sort of schema for "paint-by-numbers," that would leave no room for faith. And besides, God does not paint by numbers.

Taken from the Vital Issues booklet *Guidance*, ©1983, Multnomah Press. Used by permission.

God's Will And My Will

This study does not claim to offer all the answers for the complex decisions of life. But it does offer a plan for following what God wants you to do. Your answers to the following questions should help you evaluate your ability to make a God-honoring decision when faced with difficult choices.

- Have I asked for God's help?
- Do I show my trust for God with every area of my life, not merely this decision?
- Do I obey God's clearly revealed will?
- Am I operating on the basis of good reasons rather than changing feelings?
- Am I filling my mind with God's Word so that my mind is being transformed?
- Are there biblical commands or principles that apply to my specific situation?
- What are the alternatives and consequences of each possible option?
- How do these fare when evaluated by what the Bible says?
- Do my abilities and weaknesses have a bearing on the decision? How?
- What decision will glorify God, build me up spiritually, and edify others?
- Have I sought out worthy advisors?
- Have I carefully evaluated the advice, not merely accepted or rejected it?
- Is this decision a matter of my own freedom?
- Do I have peace that my decision is right?
- Would waiting be profitable or detrimental?
- Am I determined to obey and please God?

Discovery Series Bible Study Leader's And User's Guide

Statement Of Purpose

The *Discovery Series Bible Study* (DSBS) series provides assistance to pastors and leaders in discipling and teaching Christians through the use of RBC Ministries *Discovery Series* booklets. The DSBS series uses the inductive Bible-study method to help Christians understand the Bible more clearly.

Study Helps

Listed at the beginning of each study are the key verse, objective, and memorization verses. These will act as the compass and map for each study.

Some key Bible passages are printed out fully. This will help the students to focus on these passages and to examine and compare the Bible texts more easily—leading to a better understanding of their meanings. Serious students are encouraged to open their own Bible to examine the other Scriptures as well.

How To Use DSBS (for individuals and small groups)

Individuals—Personal Study
- Read the designated pages of the book.
- Carefully consider and answer all the questions.

Small Groups—Bible-Study Discussion
- To maximize the value of the time spent together, each member should do the lesson work prior to the group meeting.
- Recommended discussion time: 45–55 minutes.
- Engage the group in a discussion of the questions, seeking full participation from each of the members.

Overview Of Lessons

Study	Topic	Bible Text	Reading	Questions
1	Go To The Lord	Prov. 3:5-6	pp.7-11	pp.12-13
2	Understand His Principles	2 Tim. 3:16-17	pp.14-17	pp.18-19
3	Investigate Your Options	Acts 6:2-4	pp.20-23	pp.24-25
4	Discuss It With Others	Ps. 1	pp.27-29	pp.30-31
5	Express Your Freedom	Gen. 2:16-20	pp.32-35	pp.36-37

The DSBS format incorporates a "layered" approach to Bible study that includes four segments. These segments form a series of perspectives that become increasingly more personalized and focused. These segments are:

Warming Up. In this section, a general interest question is used to begin the discussion (in small groups) or "to get the juices flowing" (in personal study). It is intended to begin the process of interaction at the broadest, most general level.

Thinking Through. Here, the student or group is invited to interact with the *Discovery Series* material that has been read. In considering the information and implications of the booklet, these questions help to drive home the critical concepts of that portion of the booklet.

Digging In. Moving away from the *Discovery Series* material, this section isolates a key biblical text from the manuscript and engages the student or group in a brief inductive study of that passage of Scripture. This brings the authority of the Bible into the forefront of the study as we consider its message to our hearts and lives.

Going Further. This final segment contains two parts. In *Refer,* the student or group has the opportunity to test the ideas of the lesson against the rest of the Bible by cross-referencing the text with other verses. In *Reflect,* the student or group is challenged to personally apply the lesson by making a practical response to what has been learned.

Pulpit Sermon Series (for pastors and church leaders)

Although the *Discovery Series Bible Study* is primarily for personal and group study, pastors may want to use this material as the foundation for a series of messages on this important issue. The suggested topics and their corresponding texts are as follows:

Sermon No.	Topic	Text
1	Go To The Lord	Prov. 3:5-6
2	Understand His Principles	2 Tim. 3:16-17
3	Investigate Your Options	Acts 6:2-4
4	Discuss It With Others	Ps. 1
5	Express Your Freedom	Gen. 2:16-20

Final Thoughts

The DSBS will provide an opportunity for growth and ministry. To internalize the spiritual truths of each study in a variety of environments, the material is arranged to allow for flexibility in the application of the truths discussed.

Whether DSBS is used in small-group Bible studies, adult Sunday school classes, adult Bible fellowships, men's and women's study groups, or church-wide applications, the key to the strength of the discussion will be found in the preparation of each participant. Likewise, the effectiveness of personal and pastoral use of this material will be directly related to the time committed to using this resource.

As you use, teach, or study this material, may you "grow in the grace and knowledge of our Lord and Savior Jesus Christ" (2 Pet. 3:18).

Reflections

Reflections

OUR DAILY BREAD

Delivered right to your home!

What could be better than getting *Our Daily Bread?* How about having it delivered directly to your home?

You'll also have the opportunity to receive special offers or Bible-study booklets. And you'll get articles written on timely topics we all face, such as forgiveness and anger.

To order your copy of *Our Daily Bread,* write to us at:

USA: PO Box 2222, Grand Rapids, MI 49501-2222
CANADA: Box 1622, Windsor, ON N9A 6Z7
RBC Web site: www.odb.org/guide

Support for RBC Ministries comes from the gifts of our members and friends. We are not funded or endowed by any group or denomination.